Volume 93 of the **Yale Series of Younger Poets**

Shells

Foreword by W. S. Merwin

Craig Arnold

Yale University Press   New Haven and London

Published with assistance from the
Guinzburg Fund.

Designed by Sonia Scanlon.
Set in Bodoni type by Tseng
Information Systems, Durham, N.C.
Printed in the United States of
America by Thomson-Shore, Inc.,
Dexter, Michigan.

A catalogue record for this book is
available from the British Library.

Library of Congress
Cataloging-in-Publication Data

Arnold, Craig, 1967–
Shells / Craig Arnold ; foreword
by W. S. Merwin.
p. cm. — (Yale series of younger
poets ; v. 93)
ISBN 0-300-07909-5 (cloth : alk.
paper). — ISBN 0-300-07910-9
(pbk. : alk. paper)
I. Title. II. Series.
PS3551.R4835S54 1999
811'.54—DC21   98-31256
                                     CIP

The paper in this book meets the
guidelines for permanence and
durability of the Committee on
Production Guidelines for Book
Longevity of the Council on
Library Resources.

10 9 8 7 6 5 4 3 2 1

For John and Thomas

Contents

Foreword

W. S. Merwin

Occasionally, in the broad current of contemporary poetry and of writing about it, it seems as though an essential element of the condition of poetry—overflowing in its origin, I believe, and crucial to its survival—is in danger of being overlooked. It is the fact that poetry begins with pleasure (with "delight," Sir Philip Sidney says), and if it continues as poetry in our time, our memories, our minds, it does so as pleasure. The uneasy certainty that this is so has led the recurring waves of puritanism which our species has evolved in one repressive ideology after another (including the bottom-line puritanism of the modern world, with its gross devotion) to disparage or outlaw poetry as an undesirable and potentially hazardous substance, unprofitable and likely to encourage the notion that truth and pleasure might somewhere be related.

There is a story, probably apocryphal, from the days when the New Criticism was in flower and one of its eminences, the English critic and poet William Empson, who wrote *Seven Types of Ambiguity*, was teaching in the United States. He is said to have been impressed at the time (the 1940s) by the critical sophistication of some of the students and then increasingly exasperated to find how tenuous was the link between their analytical smartness and any personal feelings. Finally, one day he dismissed the class saying, "Don't come back until you can tell me that you have been reading Swinburne by moonlight with the tears running down your cheeks." Whatever else the story may be about—about taking things literally or not, about why students were reading poetry at all, or doing anything else—it has something to do with recognizing an allegiance to pleasure, green and not dependably correct, in which wisdom and silliness may, in fact, be present at the same time.

One thing that I found attractive, and hopeful, in Mr. Arnold's collection, *Shells,* is an unwavering fidelity to pleasure, a kind of affectionate confidence in enjoyment, in both the running chatter and the irrational magnetic rightness of the senses. This works, of course, not as a program or demonstration of a theoretical position but as the articulate response to the awareness of being present in his own skin and habits at a particular time. All the senses seem to be acknowledged here, however many there may really be, and the evocations of them range from the feeling of mussel shells under water to cooking, with its anticipations and pace and occasions and memories, to the relaying of erotic lore interlayered with friendship and the perspectives of friendship, to the uses of language, and the complex savorings and reunions of poetry itself. A resonance of freedom runs through these poems, individual, daring, at times deliberately outrageous, an air of being surprised, occasionally, at the self that is putting in an appearance, and then going on, bringing the surprise along to the party. The freedom is inseparable from the pleasure, and both are attuned to the role of form—as verse or recipes or manners or grammar—in presenting both the pleasures and the pain of mortal existence.

And so the shells of the title bespeak form, surface, outside, appearance, and last remains, and both the first and last poems in the collection—as well as many others in it— are specifically about the outer cases of lives that seem amorphous without them. The first, "Hermit crab," is a particularly elegant sonnet in which the observations and the questions raise (as the hermit crab does) further questions, including the question of how much of what seems to be known, and of what remains unknown, to the hermit crab, is projection from and of the observer. In the end the poem becomes both the hermit crab and shell:

> That's the riddle of his weird housekeeping
> —does he remember how he wears each welcome
> out in its turn, and turns himself out creeping
> unbodied . . .

And the last poem incorporates the shells (after poems
in which inhabitants of shells have been eaten, studied, vari-
ously viewed, and assimilated) into a further human shell,
an edifice, a household, a museum, all of them on the way to
becoming something else and moving on:

> He's trying to make his house into a boat,
> you guess, seeing the ship's berth where he shelves
> himself to sleep . . .
>
> . . . .
>
> . . . the tub of shells he stirs
> to recall the surf, the hall's portholes, waves
>
> painted behind, the relics on display
> like barnacles accreting on its hull.
> He walks you through them . . .

—through a mausoleum, indeed, of the outer world held still,
"slicked down with shellac," until

> Your last day—you have to leave, or live
> here forever—he gives you a souvenir:
>
> a big scrolled shell in which is still wound
> the mummy of a hermit crab . . .
>
> . . . .
>
> . . . stuck forever in the act
> of being born, an ornament, a warning.

Between the hermit crabs the poems move through
the startling indeterminate transformations of sensuous life,
accompanied by other voices, echoes, dialogue, direct address.
A number of the poems are concerned with instruction, with
telling how to do something, with practice, the practical, man-
ners, purpose, the end result of learning passed on and
through the experience, the voices, the existences of others.
"The Power Grip," for instance, in which a piece of erotic
technique is embedded in and viewed from the shifting van-

tage of a different, indistinct relationship. And "Locker room etiquette":

> bear in mind, however, that the simplest
> courtesy often
>
> is the first forgotten . . .
> . . . .
> . . . Where nakedness makes you
> shy as a hermit
>
> crab between shells, or a snail who hides his
> tremulous horns at the first smell of danger,
> summon about yourself an impenetrable
> aura, an armor . . .

The poetry, the inner life of *Shells,* is intelligent, highly wrought, accomplished, and at the same time it is a trail of exploratory motion, like those of the shelled creatures named here. The forms vary, but each poem seems to have found, or evolved for itself, a new one, and the tone, the movement of the language, its relation to speech on the one hand and musical expectation on the other, partake of the ceaseless exploration. One of the hopeful aspects of Mr. Arnold's talent is a somewhat puckered humor:

> . . . For weeks
> they take turns being sick
> —one makes tea, the other
> answers the phone. Slowly
> they can't tell better
> from worse.
> This goes on
> until one dies.
> —from "Living with it"

Shells is a gifted collection of daring writing. Mr. Arnold takes risks with abilities throughout, sidestepping niceness and easy turns. Above all, he allows poems to open out multiple reflections and leave questions alive and moving. It is hard to say what his highly individual writing may represent in the current spectrum of American poetry. It is formal without being laced into formality, assured without apparent ideology. It is on good terms with the tones of the lyric, and with the pacing of narrative and the sound of speech, and with its own "act / of being born." In the shells of this collection he is touching the raw subjects, the raw subject, with evident recognition.

Acknowledgments

Some of the poems in this book first appeared, sometimes in different forms, in the following publications:

Hayden's Ferry Review, "Why I skip my high school reunions"
New Letters, "Shore"
The New Republic, "Hermit crab"
The Paris Review, "Boots," "Amateur," "For a cook"
Poetry, "Artichoke," "Hot"
The Yale Review, "Saffron"

I gratefully acknowledge the Trustees of the Amy Lowell Poetry Traveling Scholarship, the award of which made this book possible.

To be in any form, what is that?
If nothing lay more developed the quahaug and its callous
        shell were enough.

Mine is no callous shell,
I have instant conductors all over me whether I pass or stop,
They seize every object and lead it harmlessly through me.

I merely stir, press, feel with my fingers, and am happy,
To touch my person to some one else's is about as much as I
        can stand.
—Whitman, "Song of Myself," #27

Der Mensch ist, was er ißt.
(Humanity is what it eats.)
—Feuerbach

Shells

Hermit crab

A drifter, or a permanent house-guest,
he scrabbles through the stones, and can even scale
the flaked palm-bark, towing along his latest
lodging, a cast-off periwinkle shell.
Isn't he weighed down? Does his house not pinch?
The sea urchin, a distant relative,
must haul his spiny armor each slow inch
by tooth only—sometimes, it's best to live
nowhere, and yet be anywhere at home.

That's the riddle of his weird housekeeping
—does he remember how he wears each welcome
out in its turn, and turns himself out creeping
unbodied through the sand, grinding and rude,
and does he feel a kind of gratitude?

The Power Grip

Out of the blue he calls, to report our mutual friend
    has just dumped her lover of seven years,

and why? *Because he hit her.* More than once? *She says
    it's gone on since they started going out.*

She never breathed a word . . . *Maybe she was afraid
    of what we'd think. Maybe she thought he'd stop.*

*Me, I suspect the worst of everyone — I bet
    the sex was great. I bet he gave good head.*

This should make me upset, I know, but the receiver
    is warm and round and is an exact fit

to my ear, the voice that fills it — so easy to get used
    to the liberties he takes, the indiscretion

of age, skill, seasoning. *Men don't talk enough
    about fucking,* he told me once, and leaned

closer across our table in the bar's dark corner,
    the tip of his middle finger wet, tracing

obscure designs in a pool of spilled beer. *Think
    of the slack we'd pick up if we just sat down,*

knocked back a few drinks and compared notes. His notes
    were by far the more exhaustive; he did all

the talking, the connoisseur's attachment to the part
    spare of the whole — the way bodies may be

compounded, spread out and open, made explicit,
    to grow loose, to spasm, the joints mapped,

the soft parts, their degrees of sympathy — putting
    fresh drinks into my hand, keeping up

the low murmur, seamless, fluid as Latin Mass,
    its litany *go down on her — go down*

on her again — practice, in case of emergency,
    the Power Grip. The what? He held his hands

to his face, index and little fingers thrust up, pressed
    together — this is the church, this is the steeple —

thumbs enticingly open. *Pinkies tickle the ass,*
    pointers spread the lips, thumbs for a chin rest . . .

and then as now, not knowing what or if to say,
    struck dumb, made all into one open ear.

Someday I'll get a call, some time after the fact,
    a relative, a friend — perhaps the woman

whose last bruises are fading as we speak, who won't make
    the same mistake again — but more likely

someone who knows only my rank in his Rolodex:
    He passed away last week. When I ask how,

a silence, long enough to suggest in what poor taste
    the question is. Not knowing is worse

than what I can imagine: he died of eating raw
    mussels, the ones he freely harvested

from the black rocks on the cleaner stretch of coast
    upcurrent from the harbor. He'd been warned

again and again—by beachcombers, by stray marine
    biologists, by the diehard fishermen

whose poles he found wedged between the larger pebbles—
    been lectured on dioxin and red tide,

been sick two times already, the second nearly died.
    Perhaps, instead, tipping a scrubbed clipped shell

between his lips, he breathed the wrong way, stifled
    on fringed orange flesh. I watched him once

lie belly-down on the steep pitch of a boulder, boots
    locked between the rocks, freeing his arms

to plunge, now to the elbow, now up to the shoulder
    in a tide-pool, where he knew mussels grew

thickest, their fractal clusters dark as new bruises,
    shells liable to chip, and once chipped

their insides quick to rot—a blunt butter knife
    in his right hand, the left sounding blind

under the surface, contours of curve, crevice, valve—
    Perhaps he slipped in headlong, struck rock,

was dragged out of the brine too late, or not at all,
    his body left to slowly evanesce,

the blueprint for bouillabaisse, never trusted to paper
    in twenty generations, the thin layer

of man between the brain that held it, the salt broth
    that stocked it, now dissolved. All that remains

is the Power Grip, a secret handshake, the device
    of an old cult, a rite not softened

by long use, by cultivation, a sacrament
    of which I've now been made receptacle.

For a cook

What I remember most is what he did to the couple
    who sent his best pasta back to the kitchen,

pronouncing it "too thin." Capers and kalamata
    olives tossed with squid-ink angelhair

—salty, he used to say, as sweat on a black man's cock.
    He said this often, not only to shock:

food should be made with love, and love to him was sweat,
    saliva, tears. *What do they want from me?*

he muttered, adding an egg, more Parmesan, a pint
    of heavy cream, and tossed it all together,

the straw-yellow sauce stringy with albumen,
    thickened with semen as an afterthought.

Now he is dead. I write the recipe of all
    of him that's still out there in circulation:

tips of fingers and knuckles, pared away to scars
    by the big knives, carelessly julienned

together with the root vegetables, the stray chips
    of thumbnail, here and there a curled black hair,

spit hissing in a skillet, a drop of blood in the sauce,
    the oil of his hand glazing the dough.

Scrubbing mussels

Easy at first to think they're all alike.
But in the time it takes your brush to scour
away the cement their beards secrete to stick
to the rock, to one another, you find the lure

of intimacy a temptation. Palm
cupping each shell, you learn a history
from what you scrape off—limpets, worm-
castings, their own brown crust—the company

they've kept, how many neighbors, on the fringes
or in the thick. This patriarchal shell
suffered a near-mortal crack—hinges
skewed by a scab, its valves will never seal

perfectly, ever. This one lost a chip
of its carapace—the nacre gleams, steel plate
in a war veteran's skull. Here is a coup-
le tangled by their beards—but do they mate?

You can't remember how they reproduce.
Now and then you'll find one open, startle,
fling it aside—your fingers come too close
to what you hoped would stay hidden, the veil

lining the shell, flushed pink, not orange,
no, not yet. Once they are cleaned, and more
or less alike, they're ready to arrange
in the skillet, large enough for a single layer,

with chopped onions and garlic, maybe a pinch
of tarragon—no salt, they will provide
the salt themselves—butter, a half-inch
or so of dry white wine. Replace the lid,

turn on and light the gas. Make sure the match
is thoroughly stubbed out. If you've been tempted
at any point to see in them an image
of yourself, you must make sure your mind is emptied

of all such madness. Mussels cannot mind
the slowly warming pan, the steam, or feel
real pain, which requires sympathy, a kind
of tenderness. The worst, most capable

monsters admit a feeling for the flesh
they brutalize—the inquisitors who cry
with the heretic they rack for a confes-
sion, the kind cop who stops the third degree

to offer coffee, a smoke, the death camp
doctor who celebrates a patient's birthday,
slips him an extra piece of bread—all symp-
athetic men. Think how delicious they

will be, the shells relaxing, giving up their humble
secrets, their self-possession. Your demands
are not so cruel. Don't follow their example.
Slice the lemon. Make sure to wash your hands.

Artichoke

Baffling flower, barely edible,
camouflaged in a GI's olive drab
—out loud you wonder *Who's it trying to fool?*

It is a nymph that some god tries to grab
and have his way with, I explain. She scorns
his lust, and when he sees he's met his match,
he turns her into a flower, covered with thorns
to keep her other lovers out of reach.

You say *You made that up.* You say *That's sick.*
You say *The things men think of are so cruel.*

Under the bamboo steamer there's a slick
of emerald-green water. I watch you pull
the petals off, each with a warm knot
of paler flesh left hanging at the root.

A "loves me, loves me not" sort of endeavor,
I say, but you don't laugh. It hasn't been
so long since liking me for being clever
stopped being enough for you. Sly pangolin,
endearingly nearsighted, belly rolled
up in a spiky ball—that's how I keep
my wits about me. I notice how you've polled
the petal-points an inch, how you scrape
each leaf with your incisors, the two
small grooves they leave. It makes me sick to watch.

You're awfully quiet today. What's wrong with you?

I want to tell you what . . . but there's a catch,
deep in my throat, that stops me, makes me choke
the words back, crack another pointless joke.

Saffron

The recipe is written in your voice:
Sauté the rice to the color of a pearl
in oil flavored with pepper, cinnamon bark,

bay leaf and cardamom, the small green kind.
Simmer until the spices have all floated
up to the top—if you want to, pick them out.

Just before it's done, stir in the saffron
crumbled and soaked in milk. Such frail red threads,
odd how they bleed so yellow, so contrary

to what a purple flower's genitals
should look like. It was in a dirt-poor dive
somewhere in Spain that I had my first taste

of paella—how anything could cost
so much, I couldn't bring myself to believe
until you brought me out into the fields,

the ragged sweeps of autumn crocuses.
Not like the ones I've seen breaking the frost,
clumps of three or four, with the forced cheer

of things made to wake up too early
—these were a paler purple, less audacious.
The harvesters were children, mostly girls,

working their way in no special pattern
from bloom to bloom. One of them let me plunge
my hand up to the wrist in what she'd gathered

—they felt like bird's tongues sticking to my skin,
spotted with pollen, limp, bruised and damp,
with no smell to speak of. That handful dried

would not have covered my fingernail, and that
from a whole acre. Maybe it ended up
in your kitchen, in one of the many dishes

you taught me how to make, and which we never
ate more than half of—our tongues couldn't absorb
that much, so dense and yet so delicate:

we'd dull the taste with smoke, knocking the ashes
into the champagne flutes you had shipped back
from Murano, on our way up to bed.

There can't be that much saffron in the world
—as if to think it passed through my hands twice
would make it all appear less of a waste,

that wild, endlessly nuanced fugue of flavor,
so much variety, so much to spend.
Later, at the end, when I asked you what

you wanted if it wasn't me, you smashed
the dark brown vial across the counter, swept
spice and glass into your hand and said

*This is my gold standard, my one measure
of value, the smell of money burning
—anything more expensive would be illegal.*

I couldn't even begin to afford your taste.
My fingers, stained gold with its dirty sting,
still look to me like those of a small brown hand

drifting across a field, spreading the petals,
the womb pinched out like an unsightly hair
a thousand times a thousand times over,

all for a fleeting pungency, a touch
of yellow, all to prove how much
attention you command.

The extravagance of zoos

Here in the dry consump-
tive desert, past a spray
of fountains that both day
and night are set to pump

whole reservoirs of water
straight up, in palm-tree feathers
the thirsty air withers
so quickly almost a quarter

is lost, our zoo teems
with legions of the blond
children we have spawned
to spectate, for whose games

this is an exercise
—accustomed watchfulness
will fit them to replace
their big brothers, sentries

at the frontier's most remote
outposts, who seldom wear
the regulation footgear,
or take time to vote,

but have instead married
the indigo-tattooed
natives, eaten their food,
engendered half-breed

children who play with pebble
chessmen and recite
their classics in the flat
unmodulated babble

of a second language. Lax
as we've become, we put
up with them for the tribute
they pay, by way of tax:

big wicker baskets full
of snakes, arm- and thigh-thick,
an ostrich, a rare black
leopard, a docile bull

elephant grown shabby
and ragged about the ears
from a close cage. Last year's
delivery, a baby

river-horse, recoiled
back in its box and had
to be pushed out with a prod,
trembling, into the cold

of its new mountain home.
It sat, and could be seen
most days, under the green-
corroded metal dome

(the local copper baron's
bequest) for the better half
of a year, its funny cough
much aped, its disappearance

not much noticed. But pity
is lost on the innocent,
the ingenuous, the infant
heir to some petty

title, whose first step
came only just in time
to allow him to climb,
all by himself, the steep

stairs to the guillotine,
shivering at the air
cool on his neck's clipped hair,
the raw shaved skin.

Amateur

His interest in blades of any cut
is purely amateur, he tells me. But

I know it's more than that. As he adjusts
the angle of each sword, and dusts,

and keeps the edges sharp, his keen
attention to them is almost obscene.

I like him. Thursdays we sit down to drink
—gin, on the rocks, always pink—

and I take notes, enough detail
for ten museum catalogues. He can tell

a story for each sword—where it was made,
and how it came to be displayed:

The Viking snake-sword, haft hammered
out of a twist of wire, the grain blurred

under the finish, hardly visible.
The undulating kris, so hard to pull

out of the wound it makes. The mated pair
of Hussar dueling sabers—who knows where

or in what blood they spoke their wedding vows?
The katana—a samurai would choose

a weapon, if the yellow leaves
that floated on a stream would split in halves

around the blade. If possible,
he used the body of a criminal;

it was recorded that a witty felon
wished he'd swallowed a big stone

"to spoil the edge." It must not leave the sheath
unless it can be paid a death.

He drew it, once. One night he found
a teenage burglar rummaging around

in his display. My friend asked him to leave
politely, then, perhaps, made brave

by laughter, less lightly than he'd practiced;
his first cut took one hand off at the wrist.

No second needed. After he
had bound the stump, and called Emergency,

he wiped the sword clean, set it on
the foam pads of its cradle, and asked pardon,

true to form, of the blade he'd just profaned.
He then set out to find the hand,

which took some time—the light was bad,
or else it was the several drinks he had

to calm his nerves—but when the police
arrived, he had it safely stowed on ice.

A fine story, though not one I will use.
Some evenings, when our interviews

dry up, he'll play an old record
to serenade me out. The one I've heard

the most of is the pianist
Paul Wittgenstein, "second only to Liszt,"

doing the D Concerto Ravel composed
for his left hand—he had lost

his right holding out at the Russian Front.
The notes are low, and polished black, and blunt.

Boots

Aristocrats, they were
made to walk over,
to be proud of their scars
— the bold, bare-faced upper,

the sole skinned by potsherd
or a broken Coke bottle
on the beach in Philippi
(who remembers all

the details?), the split lip
of leather, the lost stitch,
the heel caught in a throttle
and somehow reattached,

the stippled splash of bleach
from a mop, a coffee shop
in Berkeley or wherever.
The dust of half Europe

was packed into their treads
— try *that* in Birkenstocks,
see how far it gets you.
They will not learn new tricks

— imagine them plotting,
knocking back jiggers
of vodka and black pepper
with well-known figures

of the ancien régime.
High time they were retired
and quietly closeted.
Still, it will be hard

to send them packing, to hear
the snapped-together heels
stagger, or to watch
their cracked leather smiles

stiffen in disuse,
scuffing off their polish,
and each day growing
more friendly, or foolish.

Ubi sunt . . . ?

You're dead, poet who could smooth
the language like a sheet over
the body of a dying lover,
who made me realize how *soothe*

meant *show the truth*. That was the weight
you balanced lightly on your tongue.
Too young, too crude, or too high-strung,
I understand at last, too late

to tell you, how much you've impressed
on me, my brain's wet clay—your thumb
has ridged and whorled, your fingers drum
tight little rhythms still. A guest

in the House of Poetry, I slipped
downstairs at night to raid the fridge
and won the unearned privilege
of watching you, with a manuscript,

thin rows of syllables and strip
the bottom leaves of raw green shoots
to graft onto the black roots
of words—there, one firm fingertip

teases the gold leaf to lie still
along the bowed branch and the stem
of the first letter. Here's a gem
set in the ink-trussed windowsill:

a flower, a Greek name, a blue
willowware cup—all your hoard
is drawn out, piece by piece, and poured
into the hollow of a U.

Locker room etiquette

Please refrain from frankly ogling your neighbor's
penis or buttocks. This goes without saying —
bear in mind, however, that the simplest
    courtesy often

is the first forgotten. Likewise, the appraising
sidelong gaze, however surreptitious,
seldom fails to offend when it is noticed.
    Wandering eyes are

best averted. The small talk that in other
awkward situations would ease the moment
here you should avoid addressing to strangers,
    even familiar

faces, who often find it quite disarming.
This is neither the time nor place for idle
chitchat, or to broach uncertain topics —
    keep to the distance

run, the merits of this or that equipment,
warm-ups, weights, reps, heart rates, soreness of muscles.
Comments, however, on your own or your fellows'
    sweaty aroma

rarely are welcomed. Modesty and its over-
balance, in this respect, are equal, drawing
too much attention. Take, as an example,
    running the gauntlet

locker to shower, a source of so much worry.
Should one promenade the flower of manhood
fearlessly down the hall, or wear one's towel
    prudishly knotted

over the flanks, only to find it twirling
down to the ankles, forcing one to postures
neither becoming nor graceful to retrieve it?
　　Strive for a balance:

walk at a steady clip, the towel loosely
draped over the shoulder. If necessary,
practice in front of a mirror. Where nakedness makes you
　　shy as a hermit

crab between shells, or a snail who hides his
tremulous horns at the first smell of danger,
summon about yourself an impenetrable
　　aura, an armor,

over which the playful spray of the shower
spatters harmlessly. Spare the soap, and lather
only as much as may fulfill the barest
　　dictates of hygiene,

lingering nowhere long, except the armpits,
also in drying, with an unspecific
sweep over crotch, the peach-crease of the buttocks.
　　Carry your person

stiffly, as if each limb required a heroic
effort of will to flex—your head should never
drop below the armpit, or only briefly
　　tying your laces.

Handle yourself at all times with distasteful
resignation, as one regards an oyster
slick on the half-shell. Maybe it is better
　　not to imagine

oysters, or snails. Those were bad examples.
Try to forget them. Reticence in thought as
well as speech will keep your attention focused
    here in the moment,

far away from that boy on the bench directly
opposite — yes, the one that you've been sitting
naked silently beside in the sauna —
    look at your toenails,

stretch your hamstrings, think of how you are lifting
more each day, soon you'll be pressing sixty,
seventy, eighty pounds, up to the weight of
    nobody watching.

Great dark man

At quarter past midnight I meet
the great dark man. His hat is wet
—he wears a hat—and drips, as if
he's only just come off the street

into the bar out of the rain
although I know he's been here half
an hour already. He takes a stiff
drink, something masculine,

gin or whiskey double straight.
He doesn't look at me—he has
nothing to talk about. The broad
back of his hand around the glass

is dark with fur. Across the bar
I grapple with my shoe, the lace
knotted double and clenched tight
as a fist. My fingernails are chewed

too short, the lace is too wet
with rain to grip, half an hour
I've clawed at a knot as hard and grim
as ever. I turn, at last, to him.

He shakes his head silently *no*
at something I can't hear or see.
One hand closes around the throat
of the glass, the other tilts his hat

over his eyes, a helmet shut.
Tucked away in his dark greatcoat
somewhere, maybe, he has a knife.
What can't be untied must be cut.

Little shrimp

Here in a bullfight bar, the walls all black
blotches of bull and swirled red cape, I've come
armed only with the Spanish words

for *please* and *thank you* and *I don't understand*,
but they've been spent for hours. I fall back
on a German, tall blond poster boy, let

him buy me beer, let him order me
tortilla de camarónes as a joke.
Although in Spain tortilla means a deep-

dish omelet, these are fritters of tiny shrimp,
cooked in the batter whole, head, shell and all,
alive. I watch the barman mix them, pause

to catch the ones that skip out of the bowl
onto the counter, scoop them up and stir
them back in, ladle the gluey ooze

into an iron pan of oil. The German
tells me the story of two girls he met
at a disco: *One is typical Andaluz,*

black hair, black eyes, and I don't understand
a word she says, but she has better legs.
Her friend is taller, hair dyed blonde, but her,

I don't like her so much, so I go home
with the dark one. Next morning, while we two
are still in bed together, there's a knock

at the door, her friend is there with two big pans
and everything else to make tortilla — eggs,
potato, olive oil — she comes to cook

me breakfast. Now I see it's some kind
of rivalry — the other washes my clothes,
sews on my buttons. I don't understand

these girls. From his tortilla he extracts
a long orange feeler: *After you pick*
your teeth with these, yes? On the television

flamenco, fingernails instead of a pick
strumming too fast to follow. Camarón
de La Isla sings, with what little breath

is left in his cancered lungs, his face gray
from the effort — he'll be dead within a year —
his voice all in the throat, a spun-out sob,

wavering on the verge of utter tune-
lessness, at least to my untutored ear,
who thought the singers women, to the amused

uproar of all who heard me ask. Here
the women dance in dresses with polka dots
mimicking leopard, measles, ladybug.

Here, only the women dance. The men
stand by and watch, wait at the bar and drink,
clap, beat time on boxes, play guitar

or sing. The program breaks, a spot for the Pick-
Me-Up disco: men beneath black-light
dancing, their teeth glow, Cheshire Cat

grins floating—cut to a shot of two
ladybugs mating. *For those who understand,*
the Spanish caption says. I understand

the words before I think—have I picked up
more than I thought? A girl comes in, orders
coffee, looks at the German, at me, at the two

of us together, giggles, moves a little
further away on the bar. The matador
in the poster is a woman. Camarón

means *little shrimp.* A pair of small black eyes
stares back from the bitten part of my tortilla.
I'm learning to pick what not to understand.

Leader of men

Ian Curtis, 1956–1980

In all the photographs your eyes
are pale and pupil-less and look
too big for your head, your head
likewise for body. Because you're dead

we read into the frail frame
the ardor of a Bonaparte,
a *Führer* —the desire to stand
out, to be looked at. But art

and not the state took you in hand
and crushed you, the grim fame
you've massed not of a demagogue
but a scapegoat. On the first tour

the skinheads wearing National Front
T-shirts turned up. *Who is this cunt?*
they muttered at you, catching the hint,
something not altogether pure

in the way you brought the microphone
up to your mouth, the way the crowd
did not stomp or clap or brawl but stared,
the way you stared back, eyes wide

open to any suggestion. How hard
they were to penetrate, their shut
bodies, stiff fabric, asphyxiate
leather of laced-up black jackboot,

the uniform aggressive gray
—gunmetal, Prussian, mole, charcoal—
zipped, snapped, hooked, buttoned knee to throat,
faces the only spots of skin

left open, extras in a war
movie whose maker can't decide
which is more victim, whose soundtrack
is your thick voice, the epilept-

ic's rapture swallowing his tongue,
mouth a sad black hole, the young
bodies kept from each other, kept
from touching, kept from falling in.

Grace

Jeff Buckley, 1966–1997

You were barely thirty, and now you've gone
    and drowned, walked off a Mississippi

River marina in Memphis, clothes and all
    laughing, washed up at the base

of Beale Street by the bars, and you weren't even
    drunk, or like your father found

spider-clenched up with the needle still
    sticking—you, who were sweet and smart

and beautiful, who bought a hat to teach
    yourself responsibility,

dead by your own wild-child-eyed exuberance.
    The voice has gone forever out

of yourself, choked with heart stuck in the throat,
    Vienna choirboy gone banshee

dive-bombing us through thunderheads of swirled-
    together songs, the blues tuned

up too tightly, past what the wound string
    could take, snapped, a snake feeding

back on its own tail. You sang *lully lullay*
    lully lullay and got away

with it, you hallelujah'd, made me follow
    the curve of every note, led

me momently to believe. But this you leave
    to me only, to each of us

alone, no us at all—you were a vice
    as shameful to admit as chas-

tity, as embarrassing to share—like dogs
    licking a hurt we listen, womb-

walled away in our headphones, wiretappers,
    eavesdropping on the moan, mindful

not to breathe too loud, to read our own
    lips in silence. Now that you're gone,

give us the grace to slowly find each other
    out, the shed skin, the loss of in-

nocence you've been the patron of—the boy
    who lost his, tossed to one

end of a strange bed, the thread drawn
    out of his body into another's

privacy, until you lullaby'd
    him back to the sad eroded sleep

of the come-unraveled—in that husband's side
    you are a thorn, tucked into

his wife's purse next to the contraceptives,
    the one abandon he can't share

with her, played out with others, in the dark
in a parked car, unfaithful, yes,

but less than he—the girl who hounded you
from club to club, in the front row

against the stage each night, grappling the air
stretching to claw her fingers through

your head of tumbled-out-of-bed brown hair
and snare one for a keepsake,

a relic—when at last you yielded, between
Je Ne Connais Pas Le Fin

and *Last Goodbye*, groped down in your jeans,
pulled out a loose hair, tendered it

shyly for her to take. And as for me
when you washed up, I was in the south

of France, the troubadours' old stomping ground
—there, in a pink and white church,

a stopover along the Holy Bodies'
circuit to Santiago, named

for a bishop torn apart by wild horses
—there, in a crypt that smells of water

dripped through bones, is a triple box of glass,
the outermost pavilion gold,

octagonal, to match the church's spire,
the second silver, square, the last

the exact size and shape of a crack vial
    in which you barely make out

the wisp of bramble, thorn from the Thorny Crown.
    I wanted to steal the whole thing,

spirit it out of the country, take it home
    and under the tiers of glass, one

in four in eight, enshrine that single hair,
    and stick the thorn back in my side

where it belongs.

Why I skip my high school reunions

Because the geeks and jocks were set in stone,
I, ground between. Because the girls I ate
lunch with are married now, most out of spite
—because the ones I spurned are still alone.
Because I took up smoking at nineteen, late,
and just now quit—because, since then, I've grown
into and out of something they've never known.
Because at the play, backstage, on opening night
she conjured out of the vast yards of her dress
an avocado and a razorblade,
slit the one open with the other, flayed
the pebbled skin, and offered me a slice

—because I thought that one day I'd say *yes*,
and I was wrong, and I am still afraid.

Hot

I'm cooking Thai—you bring the beer.
The same order, although it's been a year

—friendships based on food are rarely stable.
   We should have left ours at the table

   where it began, and went to seed,
that appetite we shared, based less in need

than boredom—always the cheapest restaurants,
   Thai, Szechwan, taking our chance

with gangs and salmonella—what was hot?
   The five-starred curries? The penciled-out

   entrees?—the first to break a sweat
would leave the tip. I raise the knocker, let

it fall, once, twice, and when the door is opened
   I can't absorb, at first, what's happened

—face loosened a notch, eyes with the gloss
   of a fever left to run its course

too long, letting the unpropped skin collapse
   in a wrinkled heap. Only the lips

   I recognize—dry, cracked, chapped
from licking. He looks as though he's slept

a week in the same clothes. *Come in, kick back,*
   he says, putting my warm six-pack

of Pale & Bitter into the fridge to chill.
    There's no music. I had to sell

the stereo to support my jones, he jokes,
    meaning the glut of good cookbooks

that cover one whole wall, in stacked milk crates
    six high, nine wide, two deep. He grates

    unripe papaya into a bowl,
fires off questions—*When did you finish school?*

    Why not? Still single? Why? That dive
that served the ginger eels, did it survive?

I don't get out much. Shall we go sometime?
    He squeezes the quarters of a lime

into the salad, adds a liberal squirt
    of chili sauce. *I won't be hurt*

if you don't want seconds. It's not as hot
    as I would like to make it, but

you always were a bit of a lightweight.
    Here, it's finished, try a bite.

    He holds a forkful of the crisp
green shreds for me to take. I swallow, gasp,

    choke—pins and needles shoot
through mouth and throat, a heat so absolute

    as to seem freezing. I know better
not to wash it down with ice water

—it seems to cool, but only spreads the fire—
    I can only bite my lip and swear

    quietly to myself, so caught
up in our old routine—*What? This is hot?*

    You're sweating. Care for another beer?
—it doesn't occur to me that he's sincere

until, my eyes watering, half in rage,
    I open the door and find the fridge

stacked full with little jars of curry paste,
    arranged by color, labels faced

    carefully outward, some pushed back
to make room for the beer—no milk, no take-

out cartons of gelatinous chow mein,
    no pickles rotting in green brine,

not even a jar of moldy mayonnaise.
    —I see you're eating well these days,

    I snap, pressing the beaded glass
of a beer bottle against my neck, face,

    temples, anywhere it will hurt
enough to draw the fire out, and divert

    attention from the fear that follows
close behind. . . . He stares at me, the hollows

under his eyes more prominent than ever.
    —*I don't eat much these days. The flavor*

has gone out of everything, almost.
    For the first time it's not a boast.

You know those small bird chili pods—the type
    you wear surgical gloves to chop,

        then soak your knife and cutting board
in vinegar? A month ago I scored

        a fresh bag—they were so ripe
I couldn't cut them warm, I had to keep

them frozen. I forget what I had meant
    to make, that night—I'd just cleaned

        the kitchen, wanted to fool around
with some old recipe I'd lost, and found

        jammed up behind a drawer—I had
maybe too much to drink. "Can't be that bad,"

    I remember thinking. "What's the fuss
about? It's not as if they're poisonous . . ."

Those peppers, I ate them, raw—a big fistful
    shoved in my mouth, swallowed whole,

        and more, and more. It wasn't hard.
You hear of people getting their eyes charred

to cinders, staring into an eclipse . . .
    He speaks so quickly, one of his lips

        has cracked, leaks a trickle of blood
along his chin. . . . *I never understood.*

I try to speak, to offer some
small shocked rejoinder, but my mouth is numb,

tingling, hurts to move—*I called in sick*
    next morning, said I'd like to take

    time off. She thinks I've hit the bottle.
The high those peppers gave me is more subtle—

    I'm lucid, I remember my full name,
my parents' birthdays, how to win a game

of chess in seven moves, why which and that
    mean different things. But what we eat,

why, what it means, it's all been explained
    —Take this curry, this fine-tuned

balance of humors, coconut liquor thinned
    by broth, sour pulp of tamarind

    cut through by salt, set off by fragrant
galangal, ginger, basil, cilantro, mint,

the warp and woof of texture, aubergines
    that barely hold their shape, snap beans

    heaped on jasmine, basmati rice
—it's a lie, all of it—pretext—artifice

    —ornament—sugar-coating—for . . .
He stops, expressing heat from every pore

of his full face, unable to give vent
    to any more, and sits, silent,

a whole minute. *You understand?*
Of course, I tell him. As he takes my hand

I can't help but notice the strength his grip
    has lost, as he lifts it to his lip,

presses it for a second, the torn flesh
    as soft, as tenuous, as ash,

    not in the least harsh or rough,
wreck of a mouth, that couldn't say *enough.*

Living with it

It is nothing that they did
or could have helped, two people
falling in love. Not even
because they shared a toothbrush,
once. It is their germs
getting acquainted.
                        For weeks
they take turns being sick
—one makes the tea, the other
answers the phone. Slowly,
they can't tell better
from worse.
                        This goes on
until one dies.

Roommates

For Halloween he brings home a pumpkin
to carve up in front of his new girl,
a cropped-hair Kokoschka, her pared hips
too narrow for a sex—there isn't room
for one. Watching him scrape clean the skull
with a grapefruit spoon, the seeds' slippery
tangled integument, she curls her lip,
wrinkles her nose. You give her until Christmas.

■

She may not last the week—but he won't say
why. Tell me more, you say, give me the dirt.
When semen enters a relationship
everything changes. Privately you smile,
imagine the ritual: after he comes
and pulls out, he tips his little spurt
out of the rubber into a small glass vial,
capped, labeled, filed away—a name, a date.

■

The pumpkin sits out grinning on the stoop,
blotching, buckling inward into rot
until Thanksgiving. Going out he trips
over it, kicks it, loose as an empty football
into the plot of packed dirt below
the windows, a wasteland even the weeds
have given up. You sit with him and split
a cigarette, his last. It starts to snow.

■

One night you pass her in the hallway, dreary
with blood and spermicide. *You have an ex-
tra tampon? I didn't plan on staying over.*
You offer to call a cab, to walk her home,
finally hand over the cardboard tube.
Normally I use an extra-slim,
she says, *but this is fine.* You hope she bleeds
all over the sheets, all over him.

■

Spring pokes out the crocuses, and a new
sprout of something—a tendril scales the bricks,
rain-gutter, cable hookup, puts a shoot
in through the screen. The pumpkin from last autumn,
you guess, or an alien body-snatcher vine
coming to suck us dry and leave hollow
husks of ourselves. *Don't let it get inside,*
he says. *There's barely enough room for two.*

■

Each time his pumpkin puts forth a wary
yellow flower, crimped, a swell of fruit,
he snaps it off. *I'll make them into fritters,*
he says, *dipped in batter and deep-fried.*
After a week they wilt. *They'll make good soup,
maybe a minestrone.* The sodden mat
of fiber in the fridge begins to stink.
He dumps them, scours, sponges the stain with bleach.

■

You stop at a roadside stand one day and load
the trunk with cantaloupes—not smooth or green
as in the supermarket, but full-ribbed
with white mazy lace that stands out crisply.

Not waiting to get home, with the car key
you gouge one open, scoop out pulp with nails
and teeth, start the car, fingers peeling
stickily away from the steering wheel.

■

Cupping the half-shell of a cantaloupe
up to your mouth to catch the last trickle
of juice, you sit back listening to them argue
whether the brain, because mostly fat,
is sapped by diet. *You aren't going to eat
another one*, he says, seeing you reach
for the knife. *It's starting to smell like something died
in here. Could you at least take out the trash?*

■

At the first frost, the vine's entire crop
is a wizened fist-sized pumpkin, hardly worth
the effort. He'd be better off with a scalpel,
you joke. It's back to the two of you again
—they broke up a week ago, a year
to the day. The tampons disappear, the brush,
the pink plastic razors, all of the peach
nectar hair products, the shower bare.

■

Each morning when you drive him in your car
to work he rolls the windows down—the trunk
still reeks of melon, he says, still makes him sick.
Your little ritual. He hates being driven
around like this, hates having you to pick
him up, but he always asks, the familiar air
of apology for asking, as if each
time were the first, nothing ever given.

Shore

For Don Platt

On the last night of our weekend getaway
      in the beachfront house
that smells of your father's white clay meerschaum pipes,

      stems broken
after each smoke, of your mother's tennis whites
      packed in mothballs,

I lose it. When you bring to the table soup
      opaque but quickly
settling to powdery clouds, circling in the bowl's

      slow currents,
bringing up slick green squares of seaweed, cubes
      of pale bean curd,

I say, It's as if we're drinking cups of ocean.
      You can't drink
salt water, you reply. *You'd get sick,*

      see things,
not even angry, only matter-of-fact.
      When, by way

of explanation, I say the earth's surface
      and the human body
both are three-fifths water, say that blood

      was as much salt
as the sea itself, your answer then is even
      simpler: *So?*

47

I follow you on an after-dinner walk
          along the beach
in bare feet, sinking ankle-deep in the slough

          of shoreline
churned and turned, reordered and replaced,
          earth over a grave,

to watch the sandpipers steering to
          and fro, skirting
the sheets of foam that slither up, at times

          even sliding across
each other, scissorblades shearing the beach,
          and try to guess

how far each wave will reach, based on its height,
          speed, fierceness
—there's no pattern, at least not one that I

          can see, this one
falters, that one stretches its margin clear
          to the high-tide mark,

a shoal of bladder-wrack and spat-up shells,
          straw and driftwood,
bits of feather, dead crabs. When I find what I think

          is a mermaid's purse,
a clutch of shark eggs, leather-tough and black,
          and take it to you

to verify, you laugh, call it a shred
          of rubber from
a semi. *It's the same with everything,*

you say. *You make it*
something that it isn't. Why can't you let things be
themselves?

Because the sea makes all these things the same,
　　　　wearing away
the nap of the cloth, the points of the conch, the knot

　　　in the gray branch,
the hurtful jagged shard of glass, the cheekbones
　　　of a seagull skull,

grinds them all down to the tiny grains
　　　　we're letting wash
over our feet, that we're sinking ankle-deep

　　　into, losing
height, that rasp away the soles of our feet.
　　　　I try to listen

past this, past the insistence of a voice,
　　　　to make it mean
less, to hear only the hiss of white noise

　　　in a seashell,
and maybe it's just the tide's suck and settle
　　　　dragging sand

out from under my feet, that makes me lose
　　　　my balance, pitch
forward and fall, as if some swollen thought

　　　under the sand
has tried to shrug me off, as if I've put
　　　　too much weight

on its shoulders. Why did you invite me here?
        I scream.
Why do you want me around? I can't see things

        the way you do,
I can't just stand around and wait for you
        to die. *You're not*

standing, you say, holding out your arm,
        braced, leaning
away to pull me up—that's all you need,

        another body
to need pulling up. In the evening
        out of the light

the scars show up paler against your skin,
        elbow to wrist,
a constellation, twenty, though I don't count:

        the day you knew,
you went and bought a pack of Lucky Strikes,
        the first in years,

on your way to lunch with me, and after you told me
        what was what,
you sat and smoked each one down to its last

        tarred and limp
pinch of tobacco, and stubbed it out in your arm,
        and I let you.

Transparent

Kicked out of the house on Christmas Day to give them room
    to cook, we've gone to the Boston Aquarium,

my son and I, to look at fish. We have the place
    all to ourselves — the permanent displays

alone are open for browsing, though most of the fluorescent
    lights have been left off — *due to recent*

budget cuts, it says on the hand-lettered card
    taped over all the switches. A single bored

security guard, who has perhaps no family
    fussing at home, nowhere better to be

than ten steps behind, insinuates us on,
    reminding us, in the tones of a chaperone,

that *the tanks are best viewed from a distance of eighteen*
    inches — worried we'll bang the glass and frighten

the skittish fish to death, or else she doesn't trust
    the competence of fathers, thinks I'll boost

my son up for a better view of the shark tank
    and let him topple in. Well, let her think

whatever she likes. Today I've promised him we'll see
    an oppatop — his word for the plush gray

puppet I bought to distract him on his first plane ride
    — and so from room to room we skim the broad

vistas of fish, in their endless circuit against the eng-
    ine-driven current, the coral, root and branch

stupefied into stone, according to the story.
    I point things out, but it's a mystery

what will catch his attention next, what he sees
    and why: he seems to ignore the anemones'

crass colors, while the clowns that dart and couch among
    their lilac or lemon-yellow hair, unstung,

unparalyzed, make him laugh. I point out the spines
    of obscure lobsters, a see-through fish whose bones

he says are lobsters. The urchins, he can tell, are sharp,
    not to be played with. But the oppatop

squats unappreciated on a rock, turning the bale-
    ful blank of an eye toward us, and though I flail

and clap my hands, I doubt it can either hear or see
    beyond the water's limit—nothing shy

of pounding on the sacred glass will rouse the thing
    out of its torpor, to put forth a sing-

le one of its eight legs. My son has long since
    forgotten the oppatop, has no more patience

for fish he can't touch—he'd rather go home and watch
    the lights blink on the Christmas tree, switch

them on and off himself by pulling out the plug.
    Suspended in the sling, unable to drag

Daddy away, he squirms, slaps my face, kicks
    my ribs until, ashamed of my own antics,

I take him to the gift shop to buy presents—a pin
    shaped like a fish for me, for him an urchin

with flexible rubber spines. Before we can make our exit
    the guard who has dogged our heels the whole visit

catches us at the door, beckoning us to come
    back inside. —*Did you see the jelly room?*

It's new. Your boy might like it. When I look confused
    she motions us to a wing we somehow missed

on the way in, the sign from a supermarket aisle:
    Jellies. Reassuring my son that we'll

just take a quick look round, I step into a gloom
    tinged indigo, each tank a blue column,

free-standing, and big enough to hold a man
    afloat upright. I strain to read the sign:

Because of the jelly's natural transparency,
    our animals would be too hard to see

without aid. Their exhibit has been placed behind
    corrective glass, in front of a blue background,

to enhance details that otherwise might go unnoticed.
    The jellies seem enormous, almost fist-

sized, single-chambered hearts of cellophane
    merrily pumping away, water in,

water out — I had pictured them as lifeless buoys
    conducted by the tide, so it's a surprise

to see them so busy, however brainless — Freud thought
    the brain only the most articulate

fold of the skin, skin somewhere wrinkled into mind
    — a more involved jelly, now constrained

to float, with an inch of play on either side, in the skull's
    dark tank, trailing its filmy tentacles

down for a spinal cord, for nerves. What could the brain
    feel, bobbing in its warm bath of brine,

without ears, or the smaller jellies of its eyes?
    A pulse, perhaps, that liquid magnifies,

conducts directly through its sac, the filmy caul,
    the bare membrane, as when the ear canal

fills up underwater and the slightest flutter beats
    unpadded on the drum. . . . My own sight fails, the lights

cloudy, I close my eyes, open them — no — I blink
    — no — violently start forward, find the tank

right up against my nose, almost, the wild pant
    of my own breath fogging the glass. The distant

sound is my own voice, anyone's voice, chatter-
    ing at my son, explaining how the water

is really blue and not because of the detail-
    enhancing background, but a blue too pale

to see in a cup, or puddle—like the one he made
    on the kitchen floor this morning, when Grammy said

to use both hands—remember?—you can see clear through
    to the other side, it only looks blue

when there's a lot, as in the ocean, or the deep
    end of a swimming pool—the one I keep

myself from going off by spewing this inane
    babble, all that will plug the space between

my eardrum and the dumb fluttering pulse of water-
    palpitating hearts, silly, alive—*Sir,*

are you all right?—and bit by bit, I feel the jaws
    around my skull, the vise that slowly screws

my brain into jelly, loosen, until I'm brought
    by turns back to myself. The weird fit

of astonishment has passed, and now I'm terrified
    I've lost my son, dropped him, let him slide

out of the sling, his small blond head cracked on the hard
    concrete, and if he lives he will be scarred

for life, will never trust his daddy not to drop
    him again—But he has fallen only asleep,

as always when his mind has been too much impressed
    by image, form, color, needs to rest,

to squeeze the sponge before absorbing more—Freud thought
    the brain developed from the skin, not

to admit sensation but to shut it out, a load
    sometimes too heavy. I carefully avoid

the guard, her radio ready to call for backup,
    say it's time we went home, took a nap,

it's getting cold. Shoulder sore from my son's dead weight
    I stumble back at last, an hour late,

to find my mother doesn't like me anymore.
    Transparencies that no one ever looks for

aren't hard to hide, the little ways she makes it clear
    she doesn't want me around, want to appear

interested, certainly doesn't want to watch
    me doing anything, mixing a scotch

and soda, sneaking out to split a cigarette
    with *her* mother, sorting piles of wet

laundry, idly tuning the guitar a warped neck
    has made untunable. She finds make-

shift errands for me to run, sightseeing trips to see
    sights that I'm tired of seeing after twenty-

seven successive Christmases, sights that my son
    can't possibly appreciate at one-

and-a-half, all to keep me out of the kitchen, her mother's
    kitchen, where they are cleaning up each other's

messes — the crystal, rinsed in water scalding hot
    and turned rim-down to dry, is never spot-

less enough, the pans and pots not scoured, the dishes faced
    the wrong way in the washer, until they've passed

through two pairs of hands. I have to cook in secret,
    late at night, with the lights off, an omelet

whipped up in bare feet, nervous of every click
    of fork on plate. This year because I'm sick

of turkey, I've suggested lobster — which, at Mom's
    insistence, must be served with longneck clams

and big bags of potato chips, the wrinkled kind.
    I'm beginning to wish I hadn't, hearing the strained

silence within the kitchen, a storm whose eye I've stepped
    squarely into. My son will not be kept

out of the way, awake, uncomfortably aware
    that no one's talking, wants to help prepare

dinner too — and so, a cat teaching a kitten
    how to torment its prey, I entertain

him with the doomed lobsters, roll their tails out straight
    to see them snap back, test how tight

their pincer-claws can grip by hanging them from a pencil,
    until it's time to put them on to boil

and my mother wants us out. *Why don't you walk your son
    to the pond to feed the ducks?* The ducks are gone,

Mom, all of them, to Florida. They're getting fat
    on your sister's stale croissants. *But there's the fort,*

the harbor, all the boats are anchored, he might enjoy
  the boats. I remember when you were a boy

about his age, your granddad took you to the harbor
  to find beach-glass. Yes, there's still a jar

in the bathroom, one piece at the bottom cobalt blue
  so familiar I'm swamped by déjà vu

each time I take a piss. *We don't appreciate*
  that kind of language here, she scowls, too late

to stop her mother giggling. Her mother doesn't care
  —widowed at sixty, now she has her hair

done every week, last summer took a cruise to Scan-
  dinavia, tanned her still-perfect skin,

each day a wrinkle smoothed out of her brain, a lost
  memory, the names of her children crossed,

a missed turn home—I'm not sure which of these is the sin
  my mother can't forgive. We sit down

at last to a dinner of embarrassingly vast
  abundance, even for Christmas—plates of oyst-

er crackers, three lobsters apiece, impossible,
  no salad, but instead a salad bowl

of steamers, their limp necks protruding like the black
  tongues of strangled men, almost a stick

of butter each, not skimmed enough to clarify,
  quickly congealing. *Did you forget to buy*

lemons? my mother asks, but Grammy plays deaf,
     turns to me instead. *We'll save the lef-*

tovers for that bisque of yours, she says. *I hear you're quite
     the cook these days.* Does she hear my late-night

forays into the kitchen? Did I forget to rinse
     my glasses? Leave the milk out? Fingerprints

on the silverware? I swear never again. *Your house
     will stink for a week,* Mom warns her. *That's one mess*

I won't be cleaning up.—*Heaven forbid your nose
     should be offended. We'll just leave the windows*

open, won't we, dear? Not daring to look at Mom's
     face, I fix my attention on the clams,

which I quickly find were not left long enough to soak
     —washed in several waters, as my cookbook

daintily recommends—whatever part of their knot-
     ted tube of body is stomach still a glut

of fine black grit. My molars grind. I try to pass
     on a second helping, hoping Mom won't notice,

but what could I ever hide from her? *It helps to shuck
     them first. The black part of the neck*

is too tough to chew, but it slides back and off—
     She demonstrates, guesses the meaning of

my raised eyebrow—*Your grandfather called it a foreskin.*
     Her mother flashes her a not-at-the-din-

ner-table look, an admonishment she only brushes
off with a grin grown suddenly malicious.

*Remember, Mom, when Daddy used to say that clams
are kosher if they're circumcised?* She claims

not to remember, makes her seamless face a mask
of innocence. *Of course you don't. You ask*

*why we're having chips, you can't even remember
that Daddy always wanted chips with lobster.*

*No one's eating the chips. Why isn't anyone
eating the chips?* Silence, until my son,

better guest than I, obliges her, demands
More chips, more chips — face, neck, hands,

arms to elbow slick with grease, crumbs in his hair,
scattered across the tray of the highchair

my mother sat in when she was about his age.
Give him some more, he's hungry. There's an edge

in her voice I can't bear to hear, a quake, a quiver
barely held back from cracking — *Don't you ever*

feed him anything? — I don't have the stomach
to play along much more, to admit the spec-

tral presence of the absent guest, the ghost she's conjured
up with potato chips and emeryboard

clams and a lobster pot boiling over sea-foam scum,
picturing us at the aquarium

or at the pond, despite the lack of ducks—to let her-
　　self make believe we've gone together,

Granddad and I, that her mother's house is not half
　　empty. A parent's body is a life

interposed like a screen, solid, opaque, obscure,
　　between you and the imminence of your

own death—it fails, it fades, letting you see clear
　　through to the nothing you'll become. To hear

a parent crying is to feel the faintest hint,
　　however second-hand, muted, distant,

of the birth-pains you were excused the first time round.
　　Mom excuses herself, gets up, the sound

of the kitchen faucet—on, off, on
　　—and I would get up if I could to join

her, but I might as well be strapped to a highchair
　　myself. Her mother shrugs, and with an air

of abandonment takes up the claw that she has cracked
　　so expertly, picks out the meat, affect-

ing not to hear the noise in the kitchen, my mother's nose
　　blowing. My son won't touch the lobster, eyes

with grave suspicion the armor shucked onto our plates,
　　broken caskets and greaves, the doffed helmet's

twin plumes, cracked gauntlets, legs like straws
　　sucked clean of meat—I look, I recognize

my eyes in his, and my grandfather's, who had no sons,
 a blue like seawater, through a distance

only, but close, too close, too clearly they become
 cornea, iris, bubbles of watery hum-

or, windows into nothing. Now the world is shut
 up in its little box—the brain Freud thought

developed from the skin tucked in a bone tank,
 meat in a shell, octopus in ink,

voice into verse. A year from now he'll see the dis-
 jointed corpse of a roast chicken, chris-

ten it a lobster. Another year he'll hear his own
 pulse pounding in his ear, in bed alone,

be for the first time beside himself—what comfort
 will I afford him then? Around that hurt

what shell will harden? What smooth fantastic pearl
 will crystallize, outline for a world

too clear to capture shape, once he learns to see
 the frail the useless the transparent me?

Merman

The night you found me spat up on the beach you thought
    you'd save me. The green wool army blanket

you wrapped around me stifled me — out of the water
    everything's hot, and even a cashmere

mantle would've rubbed me raw, compared to the roughest
    current or buffet of my home the ocean.

I can't blame you, though, for doing what you supposed
    was best. I couldn't walk — you had to carry

me flopped over your shoulder, and by your panting
    I first could appreciate the weight of being

pulled down on every front, lifted up by nothing
    outer to self. The weak tea doubled me over,

I drank it anyway, drained too far to struggle
    —you had to hold my head steady, cradled,

crooked in your arm, your fingers idly twirling the salted
    snarls of my hair, as if I didn't notice.

At last it dawned on you to slide me into the bathtub
    with the cold water running, every now

and then sneaking a peek to see how things were panning
    out — I'd see that plastic shower curtain

rustle its big hibiscus blossom print, the corner
    turn back, one eye shyly drinking in

a spectacle of listlessness. At first you were frightened
    I'd drowned, and splashed excitedly until

I surfaced, the water's skin tickling my cheekbones,
    to explain—my first words in your weird climate,

its bleary mummifying air—that drowned corpses always
    floated face down. *So you can talk,* you started

guiltily—later, you'd tell me how you were turning
    over, in your mind, all of the silly

asides, the half-meant endearments, self-betrayals
    you might have let slip out before you suspected

I listened and understood—caught, like a mother hearing
    harsh words mouthed back by her two-year-old.

I can't say who seduced whom. You said you were drawn to
    coldness, the impenetrable mother-

of-pearl that sealed me from the waist down, a chain-mail
    iridescence. Perhaps I was a challenge.

And me? I loved your unapologetic silence,
    something to fill. I found myself telling

the silliest and—to my mind—the most transparent
    fables: *Sometimes we swim up to drowning*

sailors and wave them gently to the shore. We never
    let them see us, or we'd be hunted down

with nets, harpoons. In fact, if any of us are captured
    alive, we've sworn to die before revealing

our natures. Yes — we can will ourselves to die, dissolving
  into a yeasty froth. Your Aphrodite

sprung out of sea-foam is the land dweller's version
  of one of our oldest myths, the first mermaid

who chose to die. Unless we choose, we live forever.
  But in the end, of course, everyone chooses.

I shudder to think what might have happened if it hadn't
  been you who found me — I can trust you, can't I,

not to give me away, to keep my secret? I was shameless.
  I told you how we used pearls for money,

tended schools of fish — *just like your sheep.* You wanted
  to see the ocean's torment, the torn ruffled

surface that I myself had only known by rumor
  —I did my best, passed on myself a sentence

of lifelong exile from a grim marine tribunal,
  pictured the sad march to the utmost border,

the bellow of blown shells, the escorts armed with tridents.
  I was afraid you'd find the truth so sordid:

Under the sea we pretty much keep to ourselves.
  I almost fooled myself. Your expectations

too simple to be believed, I thought that I was leading
  —the way in bed you shivered, all the covers

kicked off to accommodate me, how I tented
  your head within my hair — it smelled like seaweed,

you said, and did I disagree? But when you opened
    your eyes out to a cold blue horizon

to take in, assume, overreach—when you declared *I'm not
    afraid of you,* I felt the agonizing

grind of loss and potential, and with my hands lifted
    up to my face, I saw how they could alter,

no longer only feeble rudders to keep balance
    but points of pain, how if I stirred the ocean

now they would frost over—and in that shrunken moment
    I would have drunk whatever magic potion

you offered me, and hauled my shimmering tongue even
    out at the root, been split up through the middle,

body torn and twinned, divided and healed over
    a form forked as the mandrake dragged screaming

out of the soil—the edge of where I could first imagine
    myself given over into a curdle

of foam, beckoned across the crests and troughs of a current
    to which all bodies in the end submit.

Watching for mermaids

Morning after cold
    morning now for years
        he hauls his telescope

out to this algae-slick
    spit of rock, props
        the tripod, turns the screws,

swabs the lens and eye-
    piece with a clean rag,
        sits and waits. Here

is the best spot, the widest
    prospect, an offshore
        wind, the whitecaps broken

down to a lap crossing
    the sandbar, a few likely
        rocks for basking, the bay

he sweeps in slow circuits,
    scans for the telltale
        flash of bare back

or shoulder, the tail raised
    in breach before sounding.
        In the sand he plants

toy windmills, red and green
    vanes chopping the breeze,
        sticks of incense, mirrors

to catch the sun, bottles,
    Coke cans—to pique
        the curiosity

for which they are of course
    remarkable. The flocks
        of gulls he gives his keen

attention, takes notes
    on where and when they gather
        and what around. Already

he's written a whole treatise
    on tail-flukes—horizontal
        like whales' and so truly

mammal. They must exist,
    because he imagines them.
        They must, because he's never

seen one. Because
    he's been so patient,
        so vigilant, they've come

to anticipate his spotting
    patterns, surfacing just
        out of his line of sight.

One afternoon a girl
    strolls past out of focus
        and in the slender drain-

pipe shimmy of her jeans
    he imagines the sleek dazzle
        of scales. *Take off your pants,*

he shouts, *I have to make*
        sure. She shrugs—why not?
                loosens her belt. Her skin

sunburned pink, her black
        lace panties, such a com-
                promise—he dashes down

to the beach, until his ankle
        twists in a dune, takes
                him down. Does he see desire

is nothing you can choose
        underwear to match?
                Or does he only collect

himself, dust off
        the loose sand, stand,
                hobble back to his post?

Some days he keeps his gaze
        trained on the same small
                circle of surf. Some days

when the fog hems him in
        he only sits, facing
                the other way, back

to the bay, training himself
        not to look back
                over his shoulder, not

to turn around no matter
        how tempting it may seem
                in the hope that one will come

slipping quietly
    as only they can
        out of the waves' chuckle

over the limpets and drooping
    clumps of weed to watch
        him for a while for

a change before chancing
    a touch, a brush, a first
        contact, a cold hand

laid gingerly
    against his arm like that
        yes   like that

Scheherazade

The porch on which we sit and drink red wine
is open, anyone could hear us, we
have no secrets, not a thing to hide.

I cross my legs, letting the instep nest
the swell of your calf, a pass you take in stride,
a first presumption, as if you aren't impressed

or not enough to move away — you pause
only to take another long drag
on the cigarette we're sharing, and pick up

the thread right where you dropped it, a long yarn
of wild high school days: *We got so high
the car was filled with smoke, we couldn't see*

*a thing. I guess the cop came by and shined
a flashlight in — I thought I'd gone blind,
it was all a big white fog. We took the chance*

*and ran — I stuck the Baggie down my pants —
opened the driver's side and hit the ground
running, through everyone's backyard, around*

*the hedge and ended up at Mike's. His dad
and mom were asleep, we jumped into bed,
covers over our heads, and couldn't stop*

*giggling. Half an hour later the cop
came by, knocked on the door, woke up Mike's dad,
asked if he'd heard anything. He got mad,*

yelled at the cop, and woke up all the neighbors
all over again. Each story blurs
into the next, and so well unrehearsed

it's easy to forget I'm not the first
to hear, how your mother beat you with a belt
for fooling with the fuse box, how you'd rather

be shocked and learn that way, by accidents
not design. The drugs, the making-out
sessions you covered for, but never seemed

to be invited to. More of the cops'
incompetence. The bottle of mint schnapps
you dropped in Lisa's Jacuzzi, her parents away

in Vegas—how the fumes cleared your nose,
how you cleaned up, finding smaller and smaller
slivers of glass, some with your feet. Because

you didn't mind the sight of blood, the idea
of injury, you thought you'd be a doctor.
How you propped up and kept alive the passed-

out drunks until they sobered. The locked-door
parties you crashed and became the life of,
the scared boys you taught to talk dirty.

The obbligato of lost and left lovers,
one in particular, who played guitar
in a band, who took you—once—out to coffee,

who then, all night, for weeks, would park his car
under your bedroom window, hang around
until the lights went out, who slipped you hot

and bothered poems, harassed you from onstage,
who, as the evening goes, is starting to sound
a lot like me. I want to interrupt,

to reassure, to say I wouldn't dream
of doing that, but then I will have slipped
my foot into the shoe that you've unlaced

maybe without suspecting it would fit,
or worried that it would, afraid you'd run
out of stories, afraid to lose your head,

afraid of what you'd learn if you heard mine.
I'm afraid too, afraid you'll tell
the same story twice—the friend who slit

her wrists the wrong direction, the one who wrecked
the car you lent and then wouldn't be held
accountable—and whether we recognize

it instantly, or only when the thread
has gone too far to wind with any grace
back on the spool, will we have been spoiled

for good, our trust deflowered, will I be left
unable to pretend I'm any more
than a convenient ear, something to drain

your excess? Lovers record each other's auto-
biographies, rehearse them till they slip
from one tongue to the other without effort,

love's history without plot or meaning,
only details, nothing paring and pruning
doesn't kill—but when I'm at a loss

except to say I like the way the hairs
flow on your forearm, fine and dark, across
the grain of muscle, not along it—there's

no history, not yet, and maybe never,
that this will start—only another story.
I feel already how your brain snaps shut,

flattens me like a box, how you will cut
me out with scissors, color me black and pink,
sketch in a few features, a big nose,

find some scraps of fabric to make me clothes,
add me to your ensemble. I should fit
in neatly—the stalker and I will start a band,

join Lisa, who must by now have shriveled
into a raisin, in the hot tub, pour,
bottle by bottle, her parents' entire liquor

cabinet in, get wasted, and invite
those boys over to join us, the wallflowers
whose new loose-tongued confidence and sass

their lovers bless silently. Perhaps
I'll find Mike, still where you left him, hiding
under the covers. How will I introduce

myself? What will I be? The one who got
away? The bad idea you caught in time?
The closet skeleton? The thing that taught

you caution? Or the melancholy boy
who sat out on the porch and drank red wine?
Whatever part you write me, I'll be pleased

just to be cast, considered worth at least
a story, however warped or skewed or flat-
tering, rapt as an infant with a mirror,

the same rapture I wish you in this tail-
swallowing tale, no more or less true
than your idea of my idea of you.

Snail Museum

He's trying to make his house into a boat,
you guess, seeing the ship's berth where he shelves
himself to sleep, a lantern with stars cut

out of its tin shutter to constellate
the darkened room, the tub of shells he stirs
to recall the surf, the hall's portholes, waves

painted behind, the relics on display
like barnacles accreting on its hull.
He walks you through them, giving a set speech

for each of the curiosities, the coins
ancient and modern, the shard of human skull,
the Phoenician jars, the bed of fossil clams

petrified writhing, slicked down with shellac,
jumbled up with the amputated limbs
of baby and Barbie dolls — a monument,

he says, to the victims of the Holocaust
— the faded photos of boats, of a blank coast
still undeveloped, the scroll covered in slant

labored cursive, a copy or a draft
of the blue-and-white tile on the town hall
that commemorates the eighteen who came back

without Magellan, before the river sloughed
silt into the port, the out-of-place
icon of the local virgin, face

her followers landlocked here like to call
a flower, ceramic cheeks all but drowned
in vestment — each stuffed fish, each bit of tack-

le, buoy and ballast with its label
neatly lettered, everything made or found
washed up on the beach, and every spare

inch of wall between them that will hold
them papered with every shade of yellow shell,
a Byzantine mosaic, seamless gold

empyrean brimming the empty space
to illustrate how God doesn't care
about perspective, depth, or the way clothes

drape the body. Forty thousand, he boasts,
and counting. Is he crazy? Sooner or later
everyone loses something here, patience,

temper, track of time, memory, mind.
Of course he remembers you, when you come back
for a second visit, even invites you top-

side, to the roof, the sign lit up by floods
to catch the eyes of sightseers above
at the town's twin palaces. Here is his workshop,

pails of bleach, paint, paste, hundreds of shells
sorted by size and shade, shark jaws
impaled on balcony spikes, gaping the air

in huge cramped yawns. Here his latest
project is hanging out to dry — skates
made to swallow their own whiplash tails,

infinite figure-eights. Later he'll paint
eyes, dabble a mouth in red, a black-
caped Dracula less frightening than the fish

suntanning to leather, the tortoise-shell
cat licking the stained plaster, the smell
of stale meat drying, the drone of flies.

Downstairs you can sit for hours, he doesn't mind
if you want to smoke, he'll find a saucer-size
scallop to put your ashes. There's so much

you missed the first time: Scraps of paper jot-
ted with dreary proverbs—*what you eat today
eats you tomorrow*—*there are three types*

*of people: the dead, the living, and those who work
on the sea*—a snapshot of a shipmate lost
at sea, boy in a sailor suit, his lips

sepia-full. At sixteen they were best
friends, shipped together—is he so old?
In his face you can't read any age, mere

laugh-lines around the eyes, skin hardly cracked.
Your last day—you have to leave, or live
here forever—he gives you a souvenir:

a big scrolled shell in which is still wound
the mummy of a hermit crab, pink tips
of stiffened claws tentatively creep-

ing out on the bald white lip, something to keep
a pharaoh company in the boat-tomb
oaring him over into obscurity,

an emblem, if you like, of soul caught com-
ing out, stuck forever in the act
of being born, an ornament, a warning.

Yale Series of Younger Poets

Other volumes available from Yale University Press

The Yale Younger Poets Anthology, edited by George Bradley

Field Guide, by Robert Hass, with a new preface by the author

My Shining Archipelago, by Talvikki Ansel

Cities of Memory, by Ellen Hinsey

Living in the Resurrection, by T. Crunk

Thinking the World Visible, by Valerie Wohlfeld

Stone Crop, by Jody Gladding

Hands of the Saddlemaker, by Nicholas Samaras

Hermit with Landscape, by Daniel Hall

Out of the Woods, by Thomas Bolt

Above the Land, by Julie Agoos

Picture Bride, by Cathy Song

Beginning with O, by Olga Broumas

Gathering the Tribes, by Carolyn Forché

■

The Yale Series of Younger Poets competition is open to Americans under the age of forty who have not yet published a book of poetry. Manuscripts are accepted only in the month of February. For contest rules, send a self-addressed, stamped envelope to The Yale Series of Younger Poets, Yale University Press, P.O. Box 209040, New Haven, CT 06520-9040, or visit the Yale University Press website at http://www.yale.edu/yup/.